ASPIRE
SUCCEED
PROGRESS

Exam Success in
Biology
for Cambridge IGCSE®
Practical Workbook

T0346899

Primrose Kitten

OXFORD
UNIVERSITY PRESS

Great Clarendon Street, Oxford, OX2 6DP, United Kingdom

Oxford University Press is a department of the University of Oxford. It furthers the University's objective of excellence in research, scholarship, and education by publishing worldwide. Oxford is a registered trade mark of Oxford University Press in the UK and in certain other countries

First published in 2022

British Library Cataloguing in Publication Data
Data available

978-1-38-200633-0

1 3 5 7 9 10 8 6 4 2

Paper used in the production of this book is a natural, recyclable product made from wood grown in sustainable forests. The manufacturing process conforms to the environmental regulations of the country of origin.

Printed and bound by CPI Group (UK) Ltd, Croydon, CR0 4YY

Acknowledgements

®IGCSE is the registered trademark of Cambridge International Examinations.

The publishers would like to thank the following for permissions to use their photographs:

The publisher and authors would like to thank the following for permission to use photographs and other copyright material:

Cover: Anna Om/Shutterstock. Photos: p5: Ron Kloberdanz/ Shutterstock; p60: Rattiya Thongdumhyu/Shutterstock; p61: Rattiya Thongdumhyu/Shutterstock; p62: Choksawatdikorn/ Shutterstock.

Artwork by Wearset Ltd, Edward Fullick, Tech-Set Ltd., HL Studios, Peter Bull Art Studio, James Stayte, Trystan Mitchell, Q2A Media Ltd., Aptara Inc., David Russell Illustration, Thomson Digital, Pantek Arts Ltd., IFA Design, Clive Goodyer, Phoenix Photosetting, and Oxford University Press.

Every effort has been made to contact copyright holders of material reproduced in this book. Any omissions will be rectified in subsequent printings if notice is given to the publisher.

Experimental skills and investigations make up 20% of the assessment weighting in Cambridge IGCSE® and are examined in Papers 5 and 6. This book will help students prepare for the practical exams. Students being able to recall the practicals they have studied in class will not be enough to get the marks. They need to be able to adapt that knowledge to new situations; find errors in practicals; plan and improve practicals. This workbook is designed to fully prepare students for success in these exams.

The exam success practical workbook:

- covers the practical skills needed for Papers 5 and 6

- allows students to develop their experimental skills

- provides a wide range of test questions to assess performance in practicals.

Contents

1. A student was preparing to investigate **osmosis** in a potato. They placed a large beaker on a digital balance.

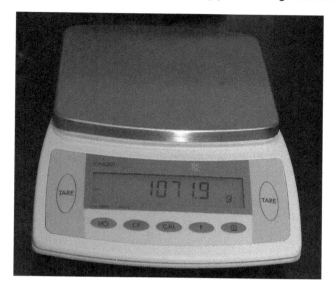

a. State what the balance is measuring.

....

.... [1]

b. Give the reading on the balance in kilograms. Give your answer to two **decimal places**.

....

....

.... [2]

c. The student records the results in a table, giving the data to the nearest whole number. Give the value the student should record in the table.

.... [1]

d. A second student used the same balance but did not return the display to zero before using it. Identify what kind of **error** this is and explain what can be done to account for the error.

....

....

.... [2]

2. A student set up an experiment to measure the volume of gas released when magnesium ribbon reacts with hydrochloric acid.

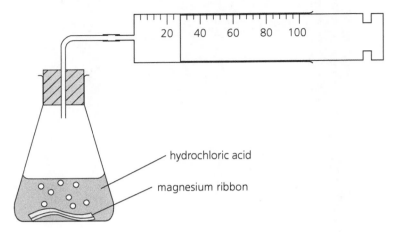

   hydrochloric acid

   magnesium ribbon

a. The student placed the hydrochloric acid in first, then added the magnesium ribbon before quickly sealing the reaction by adding the bung and delivery tube.

   i. Identify the apparatus used to collect the gas.

   .... [1]

   ii. Identify the apparatus in which the reaction is taking place.

   .... [1]

   iii. Give the volume of gas that has been collected.

   ....

   .... [2]

Exam tip

Remember to include the units in your answer.

   iv. Explain why the volume of gas collected is not equal to the total volume of gas released by the reaction.

   ....

Exam tip

Look at the method for clues.

   ....

   ....

   .... [3]

b. Suggest an alternative method that could be used to measure the volume of gas released.

....

....

....

....

....

.... [4]

3. A student measured the time taken for a drop of oil to move from a start line to a finish line.

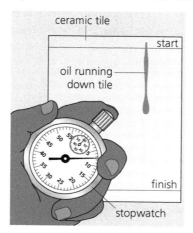

a. Give the reading on the stopwatch.

....

....

.... [2]

b. Give an appropriate piece of apparatus to measure the distance from the start to the finish line.

.... [1]

c. Two **control variables** for this experiment were the temperature and the volume of oil used in each drop. Describe how the student could control these variables.

....

....

....

....

....

.... [4]

1. A student investigated the effect of temperature on the rate of **diffusion**. They placed some potassium manganate(VII) crystals into water and timed how long it took for the colour to diffuse through the water at different temperatures.

purple colour starts spreading through the water

potassium manganate(VII) crystals

a. Identify the **independent variable** in this investigation.

....

.... [1]

b. Time is the **dependent variable**. Give an appropriate unit in which to measure the time it takes for the crystals to diffuse. Explain your answer.

....

....

....

....

.... [3]

Exam tip

This is a 3-mark question, so simply giving the unit is not going to be enough to gain all the marks. You need to explain *why* you have chosen this unit.

c. A student wants to use five different temperatures for this investigation. Suggest a suitable set of temperatures. Explain your answer.

....

....

....

....

....

.... [4]

d. Another student in the class chose to investigate the rate of diffusion at 10 °C, 15 °C, 20 °C and 25 °C.

Exam tip

Don't forget to give the units when answering this type of question.

i. Determine the range of the variable.

....

.... [1]

ii. Evaluate whether this was an appropriate range to use for the investigation.

....

....

.... [2]

e. The investigation used potassium manganate crystals. Explain how this could lead to errors.

....

....

....

.... [4]

f. During the investigation, the beaker was brought to the correct temperature in a water bath, then removed from the water bath before timing the rate of diffusion.

   i. Identify the apparatus that could be used to measure the temperature of the water.

   .... [1]

   ii. Suggest why this method might not lead to fair and repeatable results.

   ....

   ....

   ....

   ....

   .... [4]

g. The student decided to stop timing when the whole beaker was purple.

   i. Suggest how this could lead to errors.

   ....

   ....

   .... [2]

   ii. Suggest an improvement that could be made to the method to reduce this error.

   ....

   ....

   ....

   ....

   .... [4]

2. A student wanted to investigate the effect of surface area on the rate of diffusion. The student made cubes of jelly containing food colouring and placed the cubes in acid. As the acid diffused into the cubes, the cubes went colourless.

a. Explain why the acid diffused into the cubes.

....

....

.... [2]

b. Explain **two** safety precautions that should be taken when working with acids.

....

....

....

....

.... [4]

Exam tip

This question asks for two precautions but is worth 4 marks. You need to do more than just write *what* will keep you safe—*why* will it keep you safe?

c. One cube had a width of 3 cm. Calculate the volume of the cube.

Exam tip

Make sure you show all your working and include units in your answer.

.... [3]

d. A student used four cubes in a similar investigation. The cubes had widths of 1 cm, 2 cm, 3 cm and 4 cm.

Exam tip

There are no trick questions in the exam but this one is really testing if you're paying attention.

i. Predict which cube will go colourless first. Explain your prediction.

....

....

....

.... [3]

ii. The student wanted to repeat the investigation three times. Describe the advantages of repeating investigations.

Exam tip

It is not about making it a fair test; that is a common misconception with students.

....

....

....

.... [3]

iii. Prepare a table to record the results. [3]

e. Compare the surface area of one cube with a width of 4 cm and a second identical cube that has been cut into smaller cubes with equal widths of 2 cm. (You can assume that no jelly is lost in the cutting.)

....

....

....

....

....

....

.... [5]

f. A student wanted to plot a graph of volume against time to go colourless.

i. Suggest what type of graph should be drawn and explain why.

....

....

.... [2]

ii. Identify which variable should go on the *y*-axis and explain why.

....

....

....

.... [2]

g. Identify which variable should be kept constant during this investigation and explain why.

....

....

....

....

.... [4]

h. A student was provided with jelly cubes that had **universal indicator** inside them. They placed the cubes in a low concentration solution of acid and observed the colour change. Describe the disadvantages of this method.

....

....

....

....

....

....

....

....

.... [6]

1. A group of students investigated how the mass of a vegetable changed when it was submerged in sugar solution for a period of time.

   a. The students were given five different sugar solutions and potatoes. They were given whole potatoes and told to core and slice them into even cylinders. One student stated that they did not need to peel the potatoes. Another student stated that they did need to peel the potatoes. Identify who is correct and explain why.

      ....

      ....

      ....

      .... [3]

   b. Identify the independent variable in this investigation.

      .... [1]

   c. A similar investigation studied **osmosis** in carrots. Explain why the carrot cores used in the investigation need to be the same length and width.

      ....

      ....

      .... [2]

   d. The students obtained the following data.

Concentration of sugar solution / M	1	0.75	0.5	0.25	0 (distilled water)
Percentage change in mass	−39.65	−33.54	−29.34	−21.76	+12.63

      Plot a graph of the data. Use the grid below.

      [4]

   e. Estimate the concentration at which the sugar solution will be **isotonic** with the potato cells.

      .... [1]

f. Before the students completed the investigation, the teacher carried out a number of preliminary experiments to determine the best method. Identify **two** control variables that the teacher might want to determine in the preliminary experiments. Suggest a reason why it is important to use a suitable value for each of the variables you have chosen.

....

....

....

....

....

.... [4]

g. A student cut a cylinder of parsnip to use in an investigation. It had a diameter of 1.2 cm and a height of 6.4 cm.

i Calculate the volume of the cylinder. Give your answer in terms of π.

> **Exam tip**
>
> The volume of a cylinder $= \pi r^2 h$

.... [2]

ii. Calculate the surface area of the cylinder. Give your answer to two **decimal places**.

> **Exam tip**
>
> The surface area of a cylinder is two circles (top and bottom) and all the way around (a rectangle): surface area of a cylinder $= \pi r h + 2(\pi r^2)$

.... [2]

h. To carry out a similar investigation using eggs, you first need to put the eggs into acid to slowly dissolve the shell, leaving the membrane exposed. After carrying out the investigation and carefully taking all the measurements, a group of students found that the weight of the eggs remained unchanged. Suggest **one** conclusion from these results. (Assume that the students did not make any errors in their work.)

....

....

.... [2]

i. The investigation was carried out using jelly sweets. Students collected the following data.

Initial mass / g	Final mass / g	Change in mass /g	Percentage change in mass
0.92	1.35		

Calculate the change in mass and the percentage change in mass of the jelly sweet. Write your answers in the table.

[2]

j. Two groups of students carried out the same investigation but obtained very different results.

- Group A used one potato for the whole investigation. They carefully cut and weighed each sample. They ran the experiment for exactly 5 minutes then removed the samples and weighed them immediately.

- Group B used different potatoes for each sample. They only weighed one sample and used this as the initial mass for all the samples. They forgot to time the experiment. They dried the samples before weighing them.

Exam tip

In 'evaluate' questions such as this, you need to describe good things and bad things about both methods, give your opinion and state why you came to that opinion.

Evaluate the methods the two groups used. Suggest which group had the better method.

....

....

....

....

....

....

....

....

....

.... [6]

2. A student placed a sugar solution inside a visking tubing bag and securely knotted the end. The bag was then weighed and placed in a beaker of distilled water for 30 minutes.

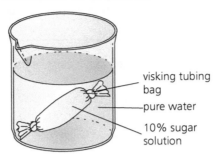

visking tubing bag
pure water
10% sugar solution

a. Explain what will happen to the volume of water inside the visking tubing bag.

....

....

....

.... [3]

b. When collecting the sample of sugar solution needed for the investigation, the student noticed that there were lumps of sugar at the bottom of the flask. Suggest what has happened and what effect this will have on the results of the investigation.

....

....

....

.... [3]

3.

○ Sugar molecules
• Water molecules

Initial level — a — Glass tubes — b — Initial level

Concentrated sugar solution

Water (hypotonic to cell)

Partially permeable membrane bags

20 °C   30 °C

a. A replica cell was set up, a concentrated sugar solution was placed inside partially permeable membrane bags to represent the cells. The water is hypotonic to the solution inside the replica call.

i. Describe how the solution inside the partially permeable membranes was made hypertonic to the water.

....

.... [1]

ii. Give a real life example where this might occur.

....

.... [1]

b. The top of the partially permeable membrane bags is not sealed shut, instead it has a glass tube.

i. Suggest the function of this glass tube.

....

.... [1]

ii. The bags were left to incubate in the water for 30 minutes. Predict what would happen to the water level after this incubation. Explain your answer.

....

....

....

....

....

.... [4]

c. The two beakers *a* and *b* are incubated at different temperatures. Predict and explain the differences you would see between the two beakers at the end of the incubation.

....

....

....

.... [3]

1. A student wanted to test a food sample to see what it contained.

   a. Describe the test for sugars.

   ....

   ....

   ....

   ....

   .... [4]

   b. Describe the test for proteins.

   ....

   ....

   ....

   ....

   .... [3]

Exam tip

Make sure you learn the names of all the food tests and reagents. In an exam, you may give the right colour change for a test but you will not get credit for your answer if you give the wrong test name. Be careful when the names of tests are similar, such as the **Biuret reagent test** and **Benedict's test**!

   c. A sample was sent to a lab for testing, but the label fell off in transit. The lab proceeded to try every test to work out what the sample contained.

Lab book	2nd August 2021
Test 1—iodine test	Result—negative
Test 2—Biuret test	Result—negative
Test 3—lipid test	Result—negative
Test 4—Benedict's test	Result—positive

   Use the information given to suggest what the food contained.

   .... [1]

   d. A student tested a 7-cm^3 sample of food for protein. The student added 1.5 cm^3 of Biuret solution A and then 2 cm^3 of Biuret solution B. Calculate the percentage of the final solution that was Biuret solution B. Give your answer as a whole number.

   .... [2]

e. Identify which of the following measuring cylinders would be the most appropriate for measuring 1 cm³ of Biuret solution. Give a reason for your answer.

- 5 ml measuring cylinder

- 10 ml measuring cylinder

....

....

.... **[2]**

f. There are four different ways to test for food groups involved in this experiment. Identify which of the following statements are true.

1. The starch test for carbohydrates goes dark brown with a positive result.

2. The lipid test goes purple if positive.

3. The Biuret reagents test for proteins needs to be heated.

Tick (✓) **one** box to indicate the correct answer.

A 1, 2, and 3 are true ☐

B 1 only is true ☐

C 1 and 2 are true ☐

D 2 and 3 are true ☐ **[1]**

g. The table lists some safety information for the chemicals used in the investigation.

Exam tip

Explain *what* can hurt you, *how* it can hurt you, and how you can *prevent* it hurting you.

Chemical	Safety information
Starch	Can stain skin
Ethanol	Flammable
Copper sulfate in Benedict's solution	Irritant
Sodium hydroxide in Biuret reagents	Corrosive

Use the information in the table, and your practical knowledge, to suggest measures that should be taken to ensure the investigation is carried out safely.

....

....

....

....

....

....

....

....

.... [6]

h. A student decided to test their packed lunch to determine what food type was in each part of a sandwich. Complete the table below to show the results. The first row has been done for you.

	Test for lipids	Test for carbohydrates	Biuret reagents test for proteins	Benedict's test for sugars
Bread	negative	positive	negative	negative
Margarine				
Cheese				
Ham				

[3]

i. Two groups of students carried out the Benedict's test for sugars. The GCSE class used end-point monitoring and looked at the colour change after 5 minutes. The A-level class used a colour probe attached to a data logger. For 5 minutes, the data logger constantly recorded the colour change and gave a numerical value for the colour change.

Evaluate these two different methods.

....

....

....

....

....

....

....

....

....

....

....

....

....

.... [4]

Exam tip

When you see 'evaluate' as the command word, your answer needs to contain very specific things. You need to point out the good bits and the bad bits of both methods, give your opinion of which is best, and then explain why you came to that conclusion.

Exam tip

A colour probe can also be called a **colorimeter**.

j. When the students in part **i** recorded the colour change at the end of the Benedict's test, this was a **qualitative** result. Using a data logger to record numerical values for the colour change gave a **quantitative** result. Explain the difference between *qualitative* and *quantitative*.

....

....

.... [2]

k. Colorimeters can be used to measure the amount of red light absorbed by a sample with Benedict's reagent in it.

Percentage concentration of sugar solution	0	2	4	6	8	10
Percentage absorption of red light	1.9	1.0	0.48	0.25	0.1	0.02

A **calibration curve** can be created using a set of solutions with known concentrations of glucose. Complete the calibration curve by:

- plotting the data from the table on the grid below

- drawing a curved **line of best fit**.

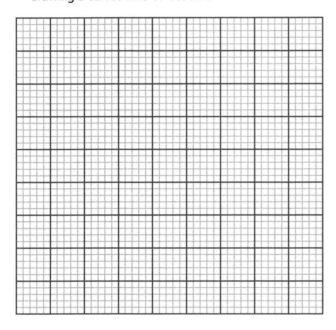

[3]

l. A student tested a range of unknown samples (A–D) for sugar using Benedict's reagent and the calibrated colorimeter. The table shows the results.

Sample	Percentage absorption of red light	Estimated percentage of sugar in solution
A	1.2	
B	0.7	
C	0.9	
D	1.5	

Use the student's results and the calibration curve to estimate the percentage of sugar in each solution. Write your answers in the table. [4]

1. A student wanted to investigate how **pH** affects the rate of an **enzyme-catalysed** reaction. They used the following method.

   Step 1 Transfer 2 cm³ of each pH buffer solution to separate, labelled test tubes. Use a separate syringe for each pH buffer.

   Step 2 Use another syringe to add 4 cm³ of starch solution to five test tubes.

   Step 3 Place the pH buffer test tubes, starch solution test tubes, and a test tube containing 10 cm³ of **amylase** solution in a 30 °C water bath.

   Step 4 Place a thermometer in one of the test tubes containing the starch solution and wait until it reaches 30 °C.

   Step 5 While waiting, add a drop of iodine solution into each dimple of a spotting tile.

   Step 6 Use a glass stirring rod to transfer a drop of starch solution to the first dimple of the spotting tile. This will be the 'zero time' test.

   Step 7 When the solutions have reached 30 °C, add 2 cm³ of the first pH buffer solution and 2 cm³ amylase solution to one of the starch solution test tubes and start a stopclock.

   Step 8 Every 10 seconds, use the stirring rod to transfer a drop of the mixed solution to the iodine solution in the next dimple on the spotting tile. Make sure the stirring rod is rinsed with water in between each sample.

   Step 9 Repeat step 8 until the iodine in the dimples does not change colour.

   Step 10 Record the time taken for amylase to completely break down the starch in a suitable results table.

   Step 11 Repeat steps 7–10 for each pH buffer solution.

Exam tip

Before you start answering the question, use a high-lighter pen to identify the dependent, independent, and control variables.

a. There are a number of different solutions used in this investigation.

   i. Describe the function of starch in the investigation.

   .... [1]

   ii. Describe the function of iodine in the investigation.

   ....

   ....

   .... [2]

b. Describe why it is important to have a drop of iodine in the spotting tile as a 'zero time'.

   .... [1]

c. State **two** variables that were kept constant throughout this investigation.

   ....

   .... [2]

d. Explain why it is important to incubate all the samples at the same temperature.

   ....

   ....

   .... [2]

e. The temperature of the starch is monitored by placing a thermometer in the test tube with the starch solution. Explain why the thermometer is placed here and not in the water bath.

....

....

.... [2]

f. Three different classes carried out this investigation. A solution of enzyme was made up fresh for class A on a Monday morning. The apparatus was left in the lab during the day for class B on Tuesday. A fresh sample of enzyme was made up for class C on the Wednesday morning.

i. The table shows the results.

pH of solution	Average time for enzyme to break down substrate / s		
	Class A	Class B	Class C
4	43	72	35
5	25	52	19
6	57	198	37
7	170	340	120

Plot a graph of the results on the grid and draw a line of best fit for each class.

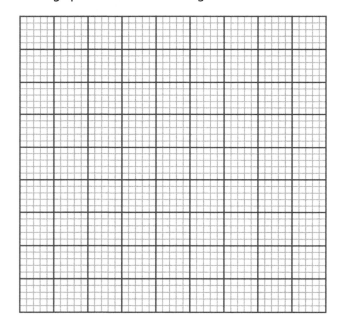

[6]

ii. Look at the results in the table above and the graph you have drawn. Suggest reasons for the differences seen in the classes' results.

....

....

.... [2]

iii. Using the graph, estimate the optimal pH for the enzyme used. Explain your answer.

....

....

....

.... [2]

Exam tip

This graph may look unusual or upside-down. Don't let that put you off. Just read the axes carefully and think logically about what the data is saying.

g. A student carried out this experiment but found that the reaction happened so quickly that even at 10 seconds there was no colour change. Suggest how the student could change their method to make the results easier to measure.

....

....

.... [2]

h. Describe why it is important to rinse the glass rod with water between each sample.

....

.... [1]

i. Suggest an alternative method that could be used to find the optimal temperature for this enzyme.

In your answer you should include:

• the apparatus you will use

• a description of how you will use the apparatus

• any measurements you will be taking

• how you will come to a result.

....

....

....

....

....

....

....

....

....

.... [6]

2. Catalase is an enzyme found in food. We can see the activity of this enzyme when it breaks down hydrogen peroxide:

$$H_2O_2 \rightarrow 2H_2O + O_2$$

hydrogen peroxide $\rightarrow$ water + oxygen

The reaction took place in a test tube and the products were collected in an inverted measuring cylinder. The following diagram shows the apparatus used.

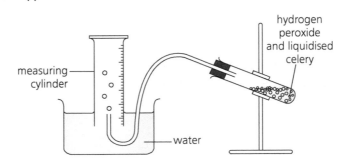

a. State which product was collected in the inverted measuring cylinder and explain your answer.

Exam tip

Think about the states of each of the products.

....

....

.... [2]

b. Two different groups recorded the data in different ways. Group A counted the number of bubbles in 2 minutes, whereas group B recorded the volume of gas released in 2 minutes. Compare the advantages and disadvantages of each way of recording the data.

....

....

....

.... [4]

c. A student wanted to record the data in the following two measuring cylinders. Give the volumes.

Exam tip

Don't forget to include units!

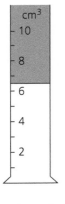

Measuring cylinder A   Measuring cylinder B

.... [3]

1. A student wanted to investigate the rate of gas exchange in light and dark situations. They set up the four test tubes shown in the diagram.

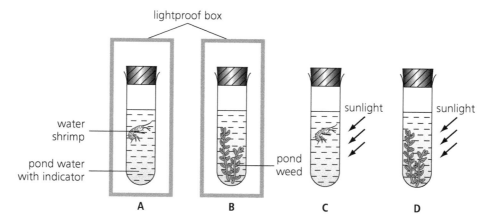

After 4 hours the student used **hydrogencarbonate indicator** solution to test the water.

a. Draw a table of the results that you would expect from this investigation. Be sure to clearly state the colour of the solution after the hydrogencarbonate indicator solution has been added.

[6]

Exam tip

Think about the biological process happening in each test tube and the products of that reaction.

b. Explain the differences in results in test tubes B and D.

....

....

....

....

....

.... **[4]**

c. The teacher suggested that a fifth test tube should have been set up without pondweed or shrimp in it. Explain why.

....

....

.... **[2]**

2. A student wanted to observe the change in pH when an acid and an alkali were mixed.

a. The student tested a sample of one solution with red **litmus paper**. The red litmus paper turned blue in the solution. State what this result indicates about the pH of the solution.

.... **[1]**

b. Litmus paper will give a qualitative test result.

   i. Explain what is meant by a *qualitative test*.

   ....

   .... **[1]**

   ii. Describe how the method could be altered to make the reaction a quantitative test.

   ....

   ....

   .... **[2]**

6 pH and the use of hydrogencarbonate indicator, litmus, and universal indicator

3. **a.** **Universal indicator** can be used to measure the pH of a solution.

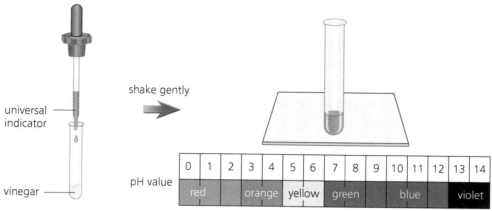

Predict the colour change that would be observed when vinegar is tested with universal indicator. Explain your prediction.

....

....

.... [2]

b. Suggest why the test tube needs to be shaken gently after the universal indicator has been added.

....

....

.... [2]

c. A student has a sample that has a pH of 12 and wants to follow the reaction as the pH increases. Comment on the suitability of universal indicator to do this.

....

....

....

.... [3]

1. A student wanted to investigate **photosynthesis**. They used the following method.

Step 1 Cut a 10 cm piece of pondweed.

Step 2 Place the piece of pondweed into a beaker of water, covered with an inverted filter funnel. Make sure the cut end of the pondweed is at the top.

Step 3 Fill a measuring cylinder with water and carefully invert it over the top of the filter funnel.

Step 4 Position a lamp exactly 100 cm from the pondweed. Switch the lamp on and leave it for 2 minutes to allow the pondweed to acclimatise.

Step 5 Start a stopclock and record the number of bubbles produced in 3 minutes.

Step 6 After 3 minutes, record the volume of gas that has been collected in the measuring cylinder.

Step 7 Refill the measuring cylinder with water and repeat steps 4–6 for distances of 80 cm, 60 cm, 40 cm, and 20 cm.

a. Suggest what question the students were trying to answer with this method.

....

....

.... [2]

b. Give a list of apparatus needed for this investigation.

....

....

....

....

.... [4]

c. Add seven labels to the following diagram to fully label it.

bubbles of oxygen gas

[3]

Exam tip

This is a science exam, not an English exam. Your answer for this should be no more than five words long. Do not answer this in a full sentence and do not repeat the question.

d. State the dependent variable in this investigation.

....

.... [1]

e. Light intensity is an important requirement for this investigation. Two groups of students carried out this investigation. One group used the light sources provided by the teacher and another group decided to use the light from their mobile phones as a light source. The two groups had very different results. Use the information in the question and your knowledge of photosynthesis to suggest why they had different results.

> **Exam tip**
>
> When 'compare' is the exam command word, you need to mention the similarities and the differences in your answer.

....

....

....

....

....

.... [2]

f. Two groups of students carried out the investigation in exactly the same way. Their results are shown in the tables.

Group 1

	Distance of light source / cm	
	10	**20**
Number of gas bubbles	120	74
Volume of gas / cm³	19	13

Group 2

	Distance of light source / cm	
	10	**20**
Number of gas bubbles	40	27
Volume of gas / cm³	18	12

Compare and explain the two sets of results.

....

....

....

....

....

....

....

.... [4]

g. Two samples of pondweed are shown below.

Comment on whether it would be a fair test to compare these two samples of pondweed. Explain your answer.

....

....

.... [2]

h. The following set of results was obtained after repeating the experiment.

		Distance of light source / cm			
		10	20	30	40
	Test 1	40	27	15	11
Number of gas bubbles released in 1 minute	Test 2	42	68	17	12
	Test 3	38	25	19	9
	Mean average				

Calculate the average (mean) of the three tests for each distance. Write your answers in the table. [4]

i. A student wanted to repeat their investigation later in the day. The sample of pondweed was first tested at the start of the day, left in water in the sun for the duration of the day, and then retested at the end of the day. The volumes of gas collected at the end of the day were much lower than the volumes of gas collected at the start of the day. Suggest why.

....

....

....

....

.... [4]

j. Suggest an alternative piece of apparatus to the measuring cylinder that could be used to collect an accurate volume of gas.

....

.... [1]

k. Describe the possible sources of error in this experiment and how they can be controlled.

....

....

....

....

....

....

....

....

....

.... [6]

I. A student investigated the effect of light intensity on the rate of photosynthesis. Their results are shown in the graph.

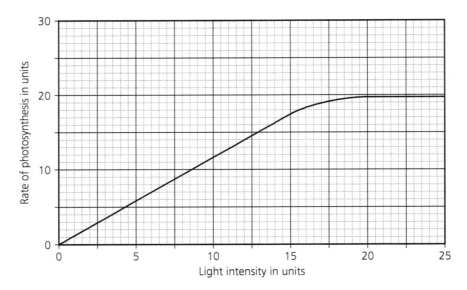

i. Give the rate of photosynthesis when the light intensity is 12.5 units.

.... [1]

ii. Increasing the light intensity beyond 20 units will not lead to a greater increase in the rate of photosynthesis. Give evidence from the graph that supports this statement and explain why this is the case.

....

....

....

.... [3]

1. A group of students wanted to investigate the effect of wind speed on the rate of **transpiration**. They used a **potometer**. The rate of transpiration is measured by how far a bubble moves along the capillary tube. As transpiration takes place, the plant takes up water and the bubble moves along. The more the bubble moves, the higher the rate of transpiration.

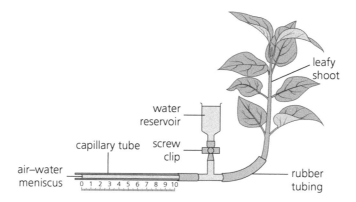

a. Suggest an appropriate unit to record the distance moved by the bubble.

.... [1]

b. Two students discussed how to takes readings from the potometer. One student stated that the distance reading could be taken from anywhere in the bubble. The other student stated that the reading should always be taken from the furthest end of the bubble. Explain who you think is correct.

....

....

.... [2]

c. Suggest a suitable method of changing the wind speed using a hair dryer. Explain why you think this method would be suitable.

....

....

....

.... [3]

d. Describe control measures that would need to be in place to ensure that the wind speed was not affected by external factors.

....

....

....

....

.... [4]

e. The following graph was drawn for the experiment.

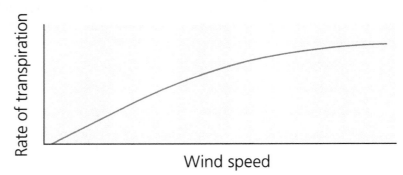

Explain why a line graph was the best type of graph for this data.

.... [1]

2. a. A group of students want to investigate how temperature affects the rate of transpiration by measuring the decrease in mass of a plant. Write a method that will allow students to carry out this experiment.

You should include:

- the apparatus you will use
- a suitable method
- any measurements you will take
- how you will use the results.

....

....

....

....

....

....

....

....

.... [6]

b. The following table was produced as a result of this investigation.

	Plant 1	Plant 2	Plant 3	Plant 4
Starting mass	22.35	21.40	35.68	19.2
Final mass	21.90	17.12		17.088
% change			−10%	−11%

   i. Complete the table. [3]

   ii. Comment on any errors present in drawing the table and recording the data.

....

....

.... [2]

   iii. Use the data from the table to suggest and explain which plant was left at the highest temperature.

....

....

.... [2]

c. The following graph was drawn.

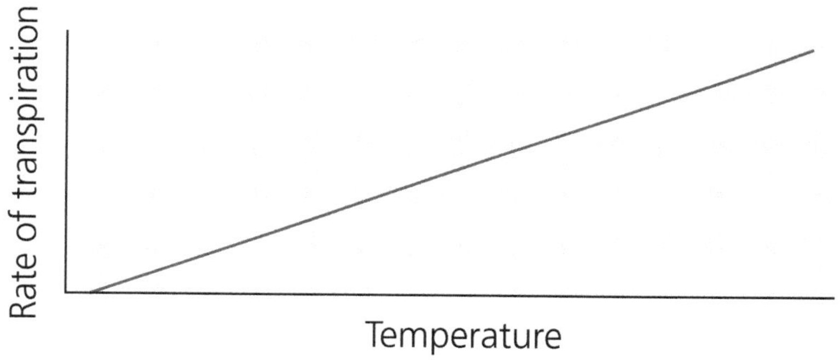

Describe how the rate of change could be found from the graph.

....

....

.... [2]

1. A group of students wanted to see the effect that physical activity had on the heart rate. They used the following method.

Step 1 Person A sits quietly on a chair for 2 minutes.

Step 2 Person B records the pulse rate of person A for 30 seconds. This is the 'before' result.

Step 3 Person A undertakes 5 minutes of exercise.

Step 4 Person B records the pulse rate of person A for 30 seconds. This is the 'after' result.

Step 5 Repeat step 4 until pulse rate returns to normal.

Step 6 Repeat steps 1–5 with different people doing exercise.

a. Explain why person A needs to sit for 2 minutes in step 1.

....

....

.... [2]

b. A student wanted to answer the question: "What effect does the length of time of exercise have on the heart rate?" Suggest an alteration to the method that would allow the student to answer this question.

....

....

.... [2]

c. An investigation compared the heart rate of two participants over time. The graph shows the results.

i. Suggest what happened at 7 minutes.

.... [1]

ii. Give the highest heart rate of boy A.

.... [1]

iii. State how long it took boy B to recover.

.... [1]

iv. Calculate the gradient of the graph for boy B between 2 and 4 minutes.

....

....

....

.... [4]

> **Exam tip**
>
> Units are key in this question—use the graph to help.

v. State at which minute interval boy A's heart rate was increasing the most. Explain your answer.

....

....

.... [2]

d. The graph shows how heart rate and breath rate per minute change during rest, exercise, and recovery stages.

Compare the differences between the heart rate and the breathing rate.

> **Exam tip**
>
> Use data points from the graph in your answer.

....

....

....

....

....

....

....

....

.... [6]

2. A student wanted to compare the composition of gas that was inhaled and exhaled. They set up the apparatus shown in the diagram.

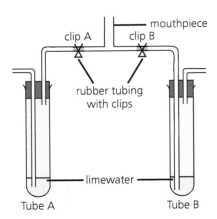

a. Describe a suitable test to determine the identity of the gas that is exhaled.

....

....

....

.... [3]

Exam tip

Remember to give not only the test but also the positive result.

b. Explain **three** precautions that should be undertaken when carrying out this test.

....

....

....

....

....

....

....

....

.... [6]

Exam tip

You should give the precaution and the reason for it.

c. Describe the expected difference that will be seen between tube A and tube B.

....

....

....

....

....

.... [4]

d. A simple version of this test will give a qualitative result. Describe an adjustment that could be made to turn this into a quantitative test.

....

....

....

....

....

.... [4]

e. The student repeated this experiment before and after carrying out some exercise. Explain what will happen to the levels of gas exhaled.

....

....

.... [2]

1. The following apparatus was set up to investigate the rate of **respiration** in yeast.

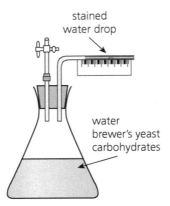

stained
water drop

water
brewer's yeast
carbohydrates

Yeast and carbohydrates were incubated in a solution. Coming out of the bung was a capillary tube with a drop of stained water in it. The reaction could be followed by the movement of the water drop.

a. Suggest why the drop of water was stained.

....

....

.... [2]

b. A student wanted to investigate how temperature affects the rate of respiration. They outlined two possible methods.

Method 1:

• **Step 1:** Incubate the yeast solution and carbohydrate solution in water baths at different temperatures until they reach the set temperature.

• **Step 2:** Remove the solutions from the water baths.

• **Step 3:** Mix the solutions and start the experiment.

Method 2:

• **Step 1:** Mix the yeast and carbohydrate solutions together.

• **Step 2:** Incubate the yeast and carbohydrate solution in water baths at different temperatures until they reach the set temperature.

• **Step 3:** Remove the solutions from the water baths and start the experiment.

Decide which method is better and explain your reasoning.

....

....

....

.... [3]

c. Suggest an improvement to both methods that would give more **accurate** results.

....

....

....

.... [3]

d. Suggest an appropriate set of temperatures to test.

....

....

Exam tip
Think about interval, range, and units.

....

....

....

....

....

....

.... [6]

e. Create a table to record the results of an investigation on how temperature affects the rate of respiration.

[4]

f. Another group of students set up the experiment in a different way, as shown here.

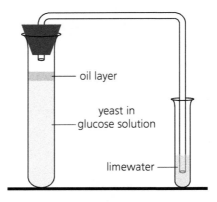

    i. Describe how this group is observing the reaction.

....

....

.... [2]

    ii. One student commented that they should place a cross behind the test tube with the **limewater**. Suggest why this might be a good idea.

....

....

.... [2]

g. Yeast solution should be made up from dried yeast.

    i. In baking it is best to do this with warm water but not boiling water. Suggest why.

....

....

....

.... [3]

    ii. The yeast solution should be used within a few hours of it being made. Explain why.

.... [1]

h. The experiment will carry on for as long as there is carbohydrate solution. Sketch a graph to show the release of carbon dioxide over time.

[4]

11 Tropic responses

1. A student investigated the effect of light on newly germinated seedlings. They used the following method.

   Step 1 Take three Petri dishes, each containing five newly geminated seedlings growing in a layer of cotton wool or compost.

   Step 2 Measure the length from the base of the shoot to the tip.

   Step 3 Using scissors, cut out one side of a box.

   Step 4 Place one Petri dish:
   - inside the box (partial light)
   - next to the box (full light)
   - in a cupboard (darkness).

   Step 5 Put a lamp or light bank above the box and Petri dishes, making sure that some light is reaching the inside of the box.

   Step 6 Add water during the experiment to make sure that the cotton wool or compost stays moist but not waterlogged.

   Step 7 Every day, for at least five days, measure the length from the base of the shoot to the tip.

   a. List the apparatus needed for this investigation.

   ....

   ....

   ....

   ....

   .... [4]

   b. State **three** control variables in this investigation.

   ....

   ....

   ....

   .... [3]

   c. White mustard seeds or cress seeds are used for this investigation. Suggest a reason why these make suitable seeds to run this investigation with.

   ....

   ....

   .... [2]

   d. State **one** problem that may be associated with taking measurements every day for seven days.

   .... [1]

e. A student grew eight seedlings in full light. They measured the height of the seedlings every day for seven days.

   i. The table shows the results. Calculate the mean height of the seedlings on each day. Write your answers in the table.

Day	Height of seedling / cm								Mean
	Seedling number								
	1	**2**	**3**	**4**	**5**	**6**	**7**	**8**	
1	2	3	4	3	2	1	3	4	
2	3	5	5	4	2	3	4	5	
3	4	6	7	6	3	5	5	5	
4	5	7	9	8	3	7	6	6	
5	7	8	10	9	3	9	7	7	
6	8	10	11	10	3	10	8	8	
7	10	11	12	11	3	11	10	9	

[4]

   ii. Calculate the rate of growth of seedling number 1 in millimetres per hour.

.... [2]

f. A seedling grew to a height of 11.2 cm over a period of six days. Calculate the rate of growth. Give your answer with appropriate units.

.... [2]

g. The table shows the results for seedlings in partial light and seedlings in darkness.

Time / days	Mean height of seedlings / cm	
	Seedlings in partial light	Seedlings in darkness
1	2.2	3.5
2	3.6	5.2
3	5.2	6.9
4	6.4	8.8
5	7.2	10.0

Plot a graph of these results. Use the grid below.

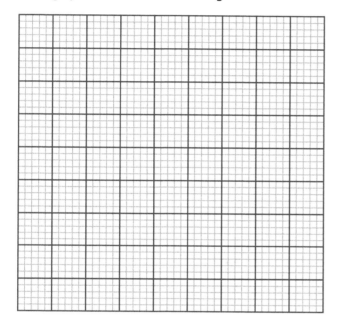

Exam tip

If you're asked to plot more than one set of data, make sure you label each line clearly.

[6]

h. A seedling was measured on day 3 and found to be 4 cm tall. It increased in height by 26 per cent over the next three days. Calculate the height of the seedling on day 6.

.... [2]

i. A group of students wanted to adapt the experiment to investigate some different variables (other than light intensity). Suggest **two** other effects of light on plant responses that they could investigate.

....

....

.... [2]

2. A group of students investigated **gravitropism** using broad beans. They used partially germinated bean seedlings so that they could see the direction of the root. The students placed the beans in a fixed position inside a glass jar. They turned each jar to a different orientation and then allowed the seedlings to grow for a further five days.

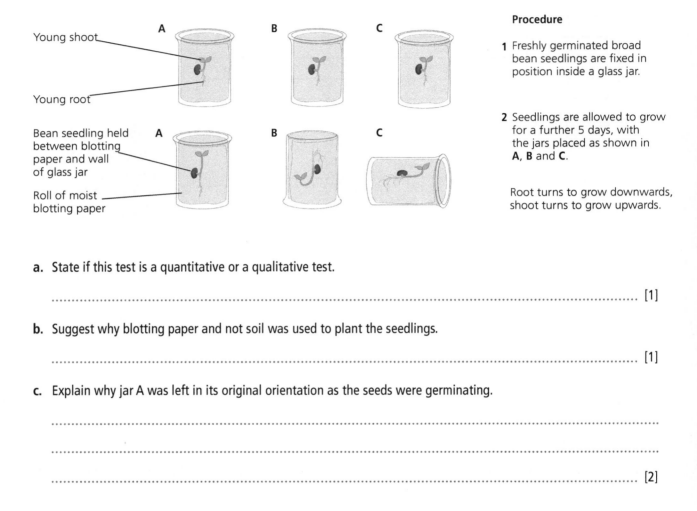

Procedure

1 Freshly germinated broad bean seedlings are fixed in position inside a glass jar.

2 Seedlings are allowed to grow for a further 5 days, with the jars placed as shown in **A**, **B** and **C**.

Root turns to grow downwards, shoot turns to grow upwards.

a. State if this test is a quantitative or a qualitative test.

.... [1]

b. Suggest why blotting paper and not soil was used to plant the seedlings.

.... [1]

c. Explain why jar A was left in its original orientation as the seeds were germinating.

....

....

.... [2]

1. A student dissected a flower to investigate the sexual adaptations of flowers.

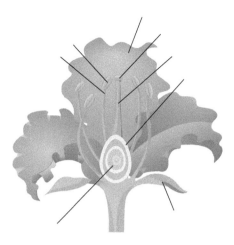

a. Draw a scientific diagram of the image and fully label it. [8]

b. Describe any safety precautions that need to be undertaken when dissecting flowers.

....

....

....

....

.... [4]

[3]

c. A student looked at pollen grains under a microscope.

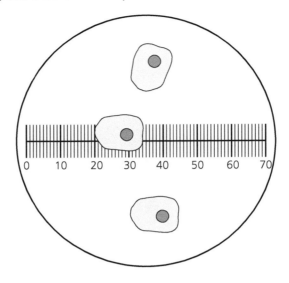

The scale you can see is in nanometres (nm). Give the length of the pollen grain.

.... [1]

2. A student studied the structure of a maize seed.

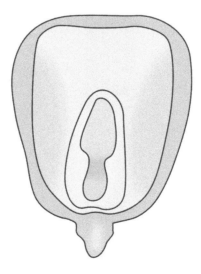

Draw a scientific diagram of the image.

[3]

1. Two students investigated the **germination** of grass seeds in a Petri dish. They placed the seeds on some wet paper and, as they were leaving the experiment over the weekend, placed a lid on the top.

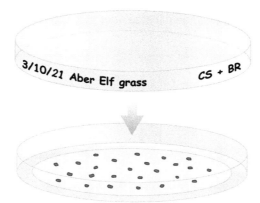

3/10/21 Aber Elf grass   CS + BR

a. Describe a method for controlling the volume of water that is added to the Petri dish. Suggest an appropriate volume of water to add.

....

....

.... [2]

b. Explain the purpose of adding the lid on top of the Petri dish.

....

....

.... [2]

c. The estimated germination time for the seeds is three days. After five days, 16 per cent of the 25 seeds had **not** germinated.

   i. Calculate the number of seeds that had germinated after five days.

.... [3]

   ii. The packet stated that the expected germination rate was 96 per cent. Out of the 25 seeds placed in the dish, determine how many would have been expected to germinate.

> **Exam tip**
>
> You do not need to have answered part **i** to try this question!

.... [2]

d. The students wrote their initials on the lid of the Petri dish, placed the Petri dish on a window sill, and left it alone at the weekend. Their teacher stated that the lid was the wrong place to write their initials. Suggest a better place to write their initials and explain your reasoning.

....

....

.... [2]

2. A teacher set up a demonstration of germination using the conditions shown in the diagram.

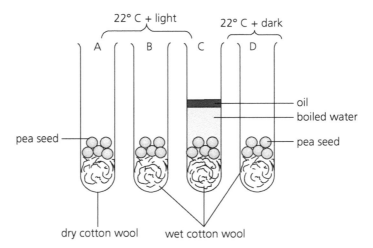

a. State which variable is being excluded at each stage.

i. A .... [1]

ii. B .... [1]

iii. C .... [1]

iv. D .... [1]

b. Suggest a suitable way of recording the results of this experiment.

....

....

.... [2]

c. Explain why five pea seeds have been placed in each test tube.

....

....

....

....

....

.... [4]

d. A group of students wanted to investigate the effect of variables other than the presence or absence of light. Describe a method they could use to investigate the effect of temperature on the growth of newly germinated seedlings.

Exam tip

If you are asked to write a method or a plan, you can use a labelled diagram to help you describe the apparatus. It only needs to be a labelled sketch so don't spend too long on it.

....

....

....

....

....

....

....

.... [6]

3. A student followed this method:

Exam tip

Use data from the graph in your answer.

Step 1   Take three Petri dishes. In each dish, place five seeds in a layer of cotton wool or compost.

Step 2   For each Petri dish add:

   1. no water

   2. 5 cm³ of water

   3. 5 cm³ of abscisic acid.

Step 3   Put a lamp or light bank above the Petri dishes, making sure that some light is reaching the inside of the dishes.

Step 4   Add water or abscisic acid during the experiment to make sure that the cotton wool or compost stays moist but not waterlogged.

Step 5   Every day, for at least five days, record the number of seeds that have germinated.

The graph shows the student's results.

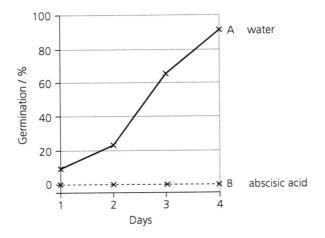

State what conclusions can be drawn from the graph and explain your answer.

....

....

....

....

....

....

.... **[3]**

14 Continuous and discontinuous variation

1. The bar chart shows the percentage of the **population** with each blood group.

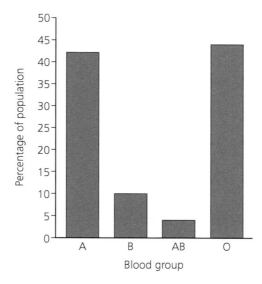

   a. State if the data shown in the graph is **continuous** or **discontinuous**.

   .... [1]

   b. Give the percentage of the population that has the blood group B.

   .... [1]

2. The graph shows the distribution of heights of 12-year-old girls.

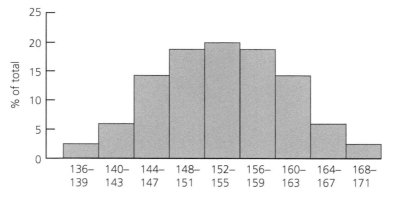

Heights of 12-year-old girls in centimetres (cm)

   a. State if the data shown in the graph is continuous or discontinuous.

   .... [1]

   b. Give the percentage of the population that has a height of 144–147 cm.

   .... [1]

   c. Identify the type of graph shown.

   .... [1]

3. This graph shows an example of continuous variation in wheat plants. All of the seeds were clones and thus identical.

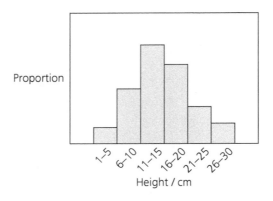

Explain why the plants' height shows continuous variation.

....

....

....

....

....

.... [4]

4. The diagram shows a variety of pea seeds.

a. State if the variation in pea seed shape is continuous or discontinuous.

.... [1]

b. Give the type of graph that should be drawn to display this data.

.... [1]

1. A class of students sampled the **population** of plants in a field. They used a sampling square (a quadrat) to enclose the area in question, and counted the samples within that area.

   This is the **random sampling** method they followed:

   Step 1   Place two 20 m tape measures (labelled X and Y) at right angles to each other to form the sides of a 20 m² square area.

   Step 2   Put two sets of cards in a bag, each with the numbers 1–20 on them.

   Step 3   Pull two numbers out of the bag. The first number indicates how many metres along tape measure X to move. The second shows how far along tape measure Y to move.

   Step 4   Place the quadrat at these co-ordinates.

   Step 5   Count and record the number of plants of the species being investigated that fall within the quadrat.

   Step 6   Repeat steps 2–5 until ten quadrats have been sampled.

   a. Identify why it is important to use a system to generate random co-ordinates instead of just choosing 'random' locations to place the quadrat. Tick (✓) one box.

   A avoids unconscious bias ☐

   B increases sample size ☐

   C faster ☐

   D reduces errors ☐   [1]

   b. Explain the need to estimate population size instead of obtaining an accurate number.

   ....

   .... [1]

   c. Calculate how many square centimetres are in 1 m².

   > **Exam tip**
   >
   > A common mistake is to write 100 cm². This is not the correct answer.

   .... [1]

   d. Another experiment used a 25 cm by 25 cm quadrat. Calculate the area of the quadrat in square metres.

   .... [2]

e. A student used a 75 cm by 75 cm quadrat to sample the school field. The field measured 30 m by 75 m. The table shows their results.

Quadrat number	Number of daisies counted
1	12
2	21
3	13
4	89
5	24
6	19
7	10
8	29
9	21
10	16

i. Use the data collected to estimate the population size.

$$\text{Estimated population size} = \frac{\text{total area}}{\text{area sampled}} \times \text{number of sample counted}$$

.... [5]

ii. Calculate the mean and median number of daisies.

Mean ....

Median .... [2]

2. A company wants to build a new headquarters on a piece of grassland that has an area of 21,000 m². The company must carry out an environmental assessment before building begins. The environmental assessment is carried out by randomly sampling ten 1 m² areas within the grassland.

a. Suggest why it is important to investigate the species in the grassland, and to estimate their population sizes and distributions.

....

....

.... [2]

b. Give an advantage of estimating population size instead of measuring the true population size in the grassland.

....

.... [1]

c. Suggest an improvement to the method that would improve the **accuracy** of the population size estimate.

....

.... [1]

1. Here is an image of *Hydrilla*, an aquatic plant, as seen under a microscope.
   Draw this image.

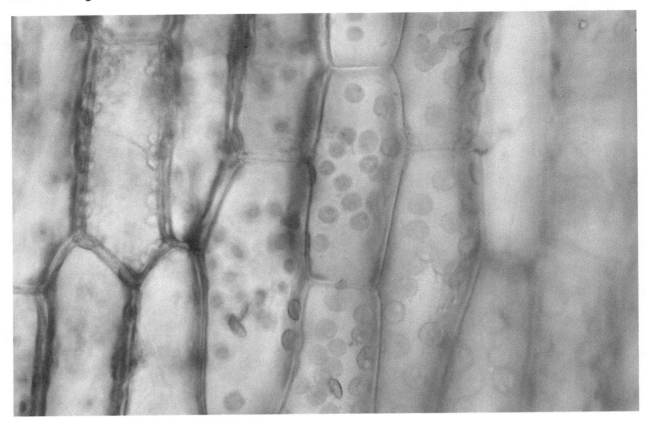

Exam tip

When drawing familiar and unfamiliar biological specimens, it is important to use clean continuous lines without any shading.

2. Draw a representative image of this sclerenchyma tissue under the microscope.

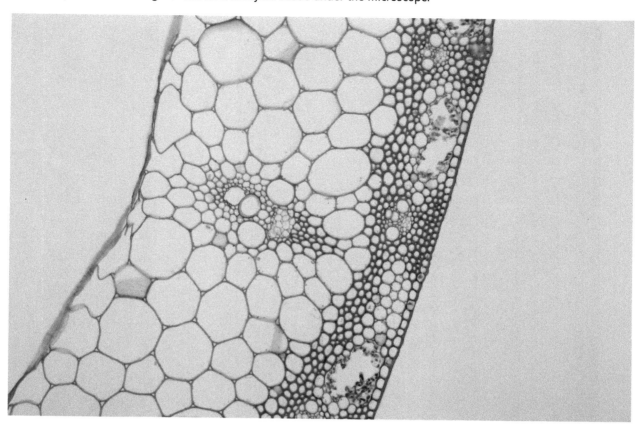

3. Draw an image of this cross-section of human tissue under the microscope.

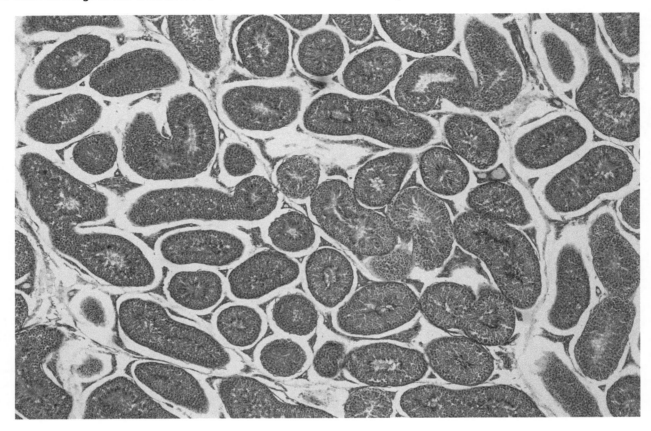

1. The following method is used to view slides under a microscope.

   Step 1   Move the stage to its lowest position.

   Step 2   Place a prepared slide on the centre of the stage and fix it in place using the clips.

   Step 3   Select the objective lens with the lowest magnification and raise the stage to its highest position.

   Step 4   Look through the eyepiece and slowly move the stage down by turning the coarse focus adjustment until the cells on the slide come into view.

   Step 5   Turn the fine focus adjustment to sharpen the focus so the cells can be clearly seen.

   Step 6   To view the object at greater magnification to see more detail, switch to a higher magnification objective lens and use the fine focus adjustment to sharpen the focus.

   a. Suggest why the slide is held in place using clips.

   ....

   ....

   .... [2]

   b. In step 3, the stage (and slide) is raised to its highest position and then in step 4 lowered as it is focused. Explain why.

   ....

   ....

   ....

   .... [3]

   c. Explain why the image is first viewed using the lowest magnification objective lens.

   ....

   .... [2]

   d. Match the part of the microscope to the function.

Slide	Part that can move around, so you can view different sections of the sample
Eyepiece	Smooth curved piece of glass closest to the sample being viewed
Objective lens	Piece of glass where the sample is immobilised and stained
Stage	Part of the microscope that you look through

[4]

2. a. A student looked at an onion cell under the microscope. This is a plant cell but it is not green. Suggest why this plant cell is not green.

....

.... [1]

b. Identify which of the following objective lenses you should start with when looking at slides. Tick (✓) **one** box only.

A ×4 ☐

B ×40 ☐

C ×100 ☐

D ×400 ☐

> **Exam tip**
>
> For this question, you need to select **one** answer. You will not get any marks if you tick more than one box, even if one of the boxes you tick is correct.

[1]

c. Explain why it important to state the magnification scale on any drawings you make from a microscope.

....

.... [1]

d. A student drew three images of a plant cell at three different magnifications but failed to label the drawings with the magnification. The microscope has three objective lenses: ×40, ×100, and ×400.

A   B   C

Draw one line from each image letter to the correct objective lens. [3]

Image A
Image B
Image C

×40
×100
×400

e. A student has prepared a sample on a slide and wants to view it using the ×100 objective lens.

Describe the steps the student should take to focus the microscope.

....

....

....

....

.... [4]

f. Put these objects in order of size, with the smallest first.

   A animal cell (10 μm)

   B ant (1 mm)

   C DNA (10 nm)

   D bacterial cell (1 μm)

   E virus (100 nm)

.... [2]

3. a. A sample was measured to be 125,000 μm. Calculate the size of the sample in centimetres.

> **Exam tip**
>
> When converting between units, the answer is going to be a 'sensible'-sized number. If the answer you get is massive or tiny, you may have multiplied numbers when you needed to divide or divided numbers when you needed to multiply them.

.... [1]

b. Magnification can be calculated by dividing image size by the size of the real object. Rearrange this equation to show how the size of the real object can be calculated.

$$\text{Magnification} = \frac{\text{image size}}{\text{size of real object}}$$

.... [1]

c. A sample is viewed using a ×4 eyepiece and a ×100 objective lens. It is measured to be 2 cm long. Calculate the size of the real sample in micrometres (μm).

.... [3]

d. The nucleus of an animal cell has a diameter of 6 μm. The diameter of the whole animal cell is 100 μm. Calculate how many times larger the volume of the cell is compared to the volume of the nucleus. For this you can assume that both the nucleus and the cell are perfect spheres. Give your answer as a whole number.

.... [5]

e. The diagram shows pollen grains viewed under a microscope. A special slide is used with a scale printed on it.

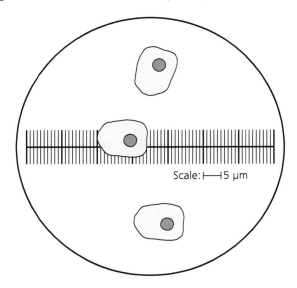

Scale: ⊢—⊣5 μm

Use the scale to identify the length of the pollen grain.

.... [1]

accuracy Reflects how close a measurement is to an actual value.

amylase The enzyme that digests starch to maltose.

anomalous result Anomalous results do not fit in with the pattern of the other results.

Benedict's test A test for the presence of reducing sugars. Benedict's solution turns orange when boiled with reducing sugars.

Biuret reagent test A test for the presence of protein. Biuret solution gives a purple or violet colour when added to protein.

calibration curve Used to determine the concentration of unknown substances based on previous measurements of solutions of known concentrations.

catalyst A substance that increases the rate of a chemical reaction and is not changed by the reaction.

colorimeter An instrument that can measure the absorption of light by a solution.

continuous variation Differences between organisms that show a range of phenotypes between extremes with many intermediates. Often results from effects of both genes and the environment.

control variable Any factor that is controlled or held constant during an experiment.

decimal places The number of digits after a decimal point in a number.

dependent variable The variable that is observed or measured in a scientific experiment. Dependent variables may change based on changes made to the independent variables.

diffusion The net movement of particles from a region of higher concentration to one of lower concentration. The particles move down a concentration gradient as their kinetic energy results in their random movement.

discontinuous variation Few phenotypes for a particular characteristic, with no intermediate forms. Typically the result of genes alone.

enzymes Proteins that function as biological catalysts.

errors Errors can be random (usually the result of poor technique—not carrying out the experiment consistently) or systematic (consistent technique but repeating the error, such as inaccurate reading of a scale).

germination Development of a seed to a new young plant.

gravitropism A response in which parts of a plant grow towards (positive) or away from (negative) gravity.

hydrogencarbonate indicator Detects changes in carbon dioxide concentration, for example in exhaled air following respiration.

independent variable The variable that is changed in a scientific experiment. Changing an independent variable may cause a change in the dependent variable.

isotonic A solution that has the same solute concentration as another solution.

limewater A solution of calcium hydroxide in water, which is alkaline and turns milky in the presence of carbon dioxide.

line of best fit Lines and curves of best fit should show an even distribution of points on either side of the line along its whole length.

litmus paper Used in qualitative detection of pH.

osmosis The net movement of water molecules from a region of higher water potential to one of lower water potential, through a partially permeable membrane.

pH Quantitative measure of the acidity or basicity of aqueous or other liquid solutions.

photosynthesis The process by which plants manufacture carbohydrates from carbon dioxide and water, using energy from light.

population A group of organisms of a single species living in the same area at the same time.

potometer A piece of apparatus designed to measure water uptake in a leafy shoot.

qualitative Qualitative data is descriptive information about characteristics that are difficult to define or measure or cannot be expressed numerically.

quantitative Quantitative data is numerical information that can be measured or counted.

random sampling Sampling technique in which each sample has an equal probability of being chosen.

respiration The chemical processes in the cell that break down nutrient molecules to release energy for metabolism.

transpiration Loss of water by plant leaves by evaporation and diffusion.

universal indicator A pH indicator, composed of a solution of several compounds, that exhibits several smooth colour changes over a pH value range of 1–14 to indicate the acidity or alkalinity of solutions.

yeast A single-celled fungus that is widely used in biotechnology as it converts glucose to alcohol and carbon dioxide.

1 Simple quantitative experiments

1. **a.** Mass
   b. 1.07 kg [1 mark for correct rounding and decimal places; 1 mark for correctly dividing by 1,000]
   c. 1.072 g
   d. Zero error; subtract the number seen on the scale from the final answer
2. **a.** **i.** Gas syringe
      ii. Conical flask
      iii. 30 cm^3
      iv. Delay between adding magnesium (start of reaction) and bung sealing the reaction; some gas will have been lost before the conical flask was sealed; not all gas will have been collected and recorded
   b. Bung with delivery tube; to an inverted measuring cylinder; measuring cylinder filled with water; measure displacement of gas
3. **a.** 8 seconds
   b. Ruler
   c. Use a thermometer to record temperature; ensure constant surrounding to make sure temperature is not a variable; use a dropping pipette or a measuring cylinder to measure volume of oil; ensure no oil is left in pipette or measuring cylinder when experiment starts

2 Diffusion

1. **a.** Temperature
   b. Seconds; minutes or hours do not have high enough resolution to see difference in rates between temperatures; any smaller than seconds would be hard to measure given standard laboratory equipment
   c. 2 marks for suitable set of temperatures: 10 °C ±5 °C (or any below room temperature but not close to freezing); 25 °C (room temperature); any other three temperatures going up in 10 °C to 15 °C intervals

   2 marks for explanation: lower than room temperature can easily be achieved with ice baths; 10 °C to 15 °C intervals are far enough apart to see a difference; range of 10 °C to 70 °C achievable in laboratory setting; not too hot that it becomes dangerous
   d. **i.** 10 °C to 25 °C
      ii. Range is too small to see any significant difference in results; the intervals between temperatures should be higher
   e. Crystals are not a standard size; each crystal has a different surface area; small crystals have a larger surface area (or equivalent); surface area will have an effect on diffusion
   f. **i.** Thermometer
      ii. No, it would not lead to fair results; as soon as the beaker is removed from the water bath the temperature will start to change; the dependant variable should be kept constant; rate changes with temperature so the rate of diffusion will not be constant over the investigation
   g. **i.** Colour will not be even throughout the whole beaker; different people will have different opinions on when the whole beaker is purple
      ii. Use a data logger; to determine colour change over time; end experiment when colour reaches certain point or percentage transmission of light at time points; reduces individual opinions
      OR
      Drop crystals in one end of a horizontal tube; determine the time it takes for the colour to travel a certain distance down the tube; narrow cut-off point; fewer errors
2. **a.** Moving down the concentration gradient; from an area of high acid concentration to an area of low acid concentration
   b. Wear goggles; to protect against splashes in eyes; wash hands after use; to prevent incidental contact onto skin
   c. 3 × 3 × 3; = 27; cm^3
   d. **i.** 1 cm cube; smaller distance for the acid to diffuse to the centre; faster reaction
      ii. To identify anomalous results; two repeats would not be enough to find the anomaly; to be able to take a mean
      iii.

Repeats	Time taken for cube to go colourless / seconds			
	1 cm	2 cm	3 cm	4 cm
First test				
Second test				
Third test				

[Units in table; appropriate headings; ruler and pencil used]
   e. Surface area of 4 cm cube = 6 × 4 × 4; = 96; cm^2; Surface area of 1 cm cube = 6 × 2 × 2 = 24 cm^2; 8 cubes in total = 24 × 8 = 192 cm^2

f.
  i. Line graph; continuous data
  ii. Dependant variable; time to go cloudy

g. Temperature; control variable; fair test; rate of diffusion varies with temperature

h. Universal indicator is green in neutral solution; universal indicator is red in acid; hard to see colour change in 3D cube; hard to accurately judge end point as it will be internal to cube and obscured by other; lead to errors; no longer a fair test

3 Osmosis

1. a. Potato does need to be peeled; skin will have different rates of osmosis; will affect the results/ not controlled/not fair test

b. Concentration of sugar solution (mention of *concentration* is needed for mark)

c. So they all have the same surface area; control/fair test

d.

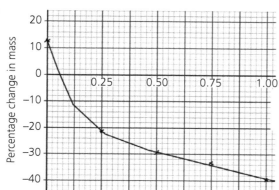

[1 mark for appropriate scale and label on *x*-axis; 1 mark for appropriate scale on *y*-axis; 1 mark for at least eight of the points plotted correctly; 1 mark for correct line of best fit]

e. 0.06 ± 0.01

f. Two from the following list or other sensible suggestion [only 2 marks can be gained from suggestion of things to test in a preliminary experiment, the other 2 marks are for justifications]:
- Time to leave sample in sugar solution; too short—won't see any change, too long— unrealistic time scale for lesson
- Range of sugar solutions; too small or too large—won't get any meaningful data
- Interval of concentration of solutions; too close together—won't see any change, too far apart—won't get any meaningful data
- Size of potato; too small—hard to work with, too large—won't fit in boiling tube

g.
  i. Radius = 1.2 / 2 = 0.6; volume = $\pi \times 0.6^2 \times 6.4$ = 2.3π
  ii. 26.39 to 2 d.p. [26.38 gains 1 mark]

h. No net movement of water (do not credit 'no osmosis took place', there is always movement of water but in this case as much went in as came out); solution was isotonic to egg

i. 0.43 g; +47% [mark only given if correct sign is used]

j. To gain full marks on the question it must be balanced between good and bad points for each group, give an opinion, and justify that opinion:
- Group A good points: control for potato, controlled for surface area of sample, controlled for time in solution
- Group A bad points: didn't dry sample before weighing so will introduce errors
- Group B bad points: no controls
- Group B good points: dry sample before weighing so they didn't introduce an error
- Group A had the better method as they had more controls

2. a. Volume increases; solute concentration higher inside bag; water moves from less concentrated to more concentrated solution in the bag

b. Not all the sugar has been dissolved; solution is not the correct concentration; results won't be correct

3. a.
  i. Adding in sugar
  ii. Roots / occasionally blood

b.
  i. To see the level of the water
  ii. Water levels would rise; increased volume of water in bag; osmosis; water would move into the bag as the external solution is hypotonic to the cell

c. higher water level in tube b; movement is faster at higher temperatures; more water will have moved by osmosis into the bag

4 Food tests

1. a. Place a small amount of food in a test tube; add enough Benedict's solution to cover the food; place the test tube in a warm water bath for 10 minutes; blue Benedict's solution turns brick red on heating if a sugar such as glucose is present

b. Place a small amount of food in a test tube; add 1 cm³ of Biuret reagent; alternatively, add 1 cm³ of sodium hydroxide solution and then add a few drops of copper sulfate solution; blue Biuret reagent turns purple if protein is present

c. Sample has sugar in it

d. $7 + 1.5 + 2 = 10.5\,cm^3$; $2 / 10.5 \times 100 = 19\%$

e. 5 ml cylinder; will be more precise for small volumes

f. B—1 only is true

g. Three from the following [2 marks per hazard—1 for hazard and 1 for associated safety measure; 6 marks cannot be scored from just listing six hazards]:
- Bunsen burner—can cause burns; inform teacher and keep burn under cold running water
- Glass—broken glass can cause cuts; inform teacher of any breakages, do not attempt to clear up yourself, seek first aid if required
- Copper sulfate—harmful if swallowed; inform teacher if swallowed and seek first aid
- Ethanol—flammable; keep away from flames, inform teacher if fire or burns occur and seek first aid
- Iodine—stains skin; wear gloves and inform teacher of any contact to skin
- Sodium hydroxide—irritant to skin; inform teacher if on skin and seek first aid

h.

	Test for lipids	Test for carbohydrates	Biuret reagents test for proteins	Benedict's test for sugars
Bread	negative	positive	negative	negative
Margarine	positive	negative	negative	negative
Cheese	positive	negative	positive	negative
Ham	negative	negative	positive	negative

[1 mark for each correct row; allow one wrong answer]

i. [Answer must be balanced with positives and negatives for each method; full marks can only be achieved if a justified opinion as to the best method is given]
- Positives of GCSE students' method—readily available equipment
- Negatives of GCSE students' method—colour change is subject to opinions and may be classified differently by different people
- Positives of A-level students' method—exact values for results; computer-monitored so little room for error
- Negatives of A-level students' method—expensive equipment

j. Qualitative is based on appearance; quantitative can be defined by numbers

k. All plotted correctly (± ½ square); award 1 mark for 4 or 5 points correct; curved line of best fit

l. [1 mark for each correct answer]

Sample	Percentage absorption of red light	Estimated percentage of sugar in solution
A	1.2	1.5–2
B	0.7	3
C	0.9	2.5–3
D	1.5	1

5 Enzymes

1. a. i. Starch is the substrate
      ii. Iodine is the indicator; black/brown for starch, yellow/brown for sugars when substrate has been catalysed

   b. A control/to have something to compare results against

   c. Any two from: temperature; concentration of starch; volume of starch

   d. To control for temperature; temperature could affect the rate of reaction

   e. To get an accurate reading of the solution; the solution might not have heated up fully

   f. i. Results correctly plotted (±½ square) for each class (1 mark for each correct class); curved line of best fit drawn for each class (1 mark for each correct class)
      ii. Difference between A and B—enzyme lost activity over the course of the day; difference between A/B and C—different solution of enzyme (may be higher concentration)
      iii. pH 5; shortest time taken for all three classes

   g. Any two from: dilute the enzyme solution; reduce substrate concentration; lower temperature

   h. So samples are not contaminated

   i. Apparatus [at least 1 mark must come from this section]
      Method [a maximum of 3 marks can be gained from this section]:
      - a range of temperatures must be tested (minimum five)
      - range of temperatures, must include one below 25 °C, one at 25 °C, and one above 25 °C
      - controlled volume of starch solution, pH buffer, iodine
      - controlled concentration of starch solution

- wear goggles and state how to carry out experiment safely
  Measurements [at least 1 mark must come from this section]:
- record the time it takes for a colour change
  Results [at least 1 mark must come from this section]:
- the highest enzyme activity will be when the colour change is fastest

2. **a.** Oxygen; it's a gas
   b. Answer must include advantages and disadvantages for each group to gain full marks:
   - Group A advantages: no need for specialised equipment
   - Group A disadvantages: less accurate; size of bubble is variable, not all bubbles contain an equal volume of gas; bubble might be too fast to count accurately
   - Group B advantages: accurate volume; quantitative
   - Group B disadvantages: potential source of error if air gap in measuring cylinder at start
   c. A—6.5 cm^3; B—10 cm^3; 1 mark for units

6 pH and the use of hydrogencarbonate indicator

1. **a.**

Tube	Colour of hydrogencarbonate indicator solution
A	Purple
B	Purple
C	Purple
D	Orange

[2 marks for structure of table; 1 mark each for result]

   b. Tube B is undergoing respiration in the absence of light; reducing the levels of carbon dioxide; Tube D in the light is undergoing photosynthesis; increasing the levels of carbon dioxide
   c. As a control; to compare the colours against
2. **a.** Alkaline
   b. **i.** Gives a yes or no result
   ii. Use a pH probe or data logger; given numbers
3. **a.** Turns orange; because vinegar is acidic/has pH 2–3
   b. To mix the vinegar and universal indicator; to see a clear colour change
   c. Not suitable; pH 12 is dark blue and pH 14 is very dark blue; change is too hard to see accurately/colours are too similar

7 Photosynthesis

1. **a.** The effect of light intensity; on the rate of photosynthesis
   b. $\frac{1}{2}$ mark each: pondweed; scissors; lamp; large beaker; filter funnel; 10 cm^3 measuring cylinder; metre ruler; stopclock
   c. $\frac{1}{2}$ mark for each correct label: metre rule, lamp/light source; beaker; measuring cylinder; water; pondweed; funnel
   d. Number of bubbles/volume of gas (use of the word 'amount' not detailed enough to gain marks)
   e. Light from mobile phone will not put out enough light intensity/different light intensity; rates of photosynthesis will be lower/none due to different levels of light intensity
   f. Same volume of gas released in each experiment; different numbers of bubbles; volume of bubbles different; group 1 had an average of 0.16 cm^3 to 0.18 cm^3 of gas in each bubble (any number in range will gain mark); group 2 had an average of 0.44 cm^3 to 0.45 cm^3 of gas in each bubble (any number in range will gain mark)
   g. Not a fair test; different number of leaves/surface areas/number of cells to perform photosynthesis
   h.

		Distance of light source / cm			
		10	20	30	40
Number of gas bubbles released in 1 minute	Test 1	40	27	15	11
	Test 2	42	68	17	12
	Test 3	38	25	19	9
	Mean average	40	26	17	11

[For 20 cm: 40 bubbles does not score a mark as the anomalous result has been included in the average; for 40 cm: 10 cm does not score a mark as the rounding is incorrect; 1 mark for each correct answer]

   i. Carbon dioxide is needed for photosynthesis; carbon dioxide is dissolved in water; at the end of the day all the carbon dioxide will have been used up, due to a day of photosynthesis; less photosynthesis will happen at the end of the day
   j. Gas syringe OR burette
   k. Bubbles being on leaf before experiment starts—gently shake the leaf to dislodge any bubble before experiment starts; level of carbon dioxide in the

water too low—add sodium hydrogencarbonate to increase levels of carbon dioxide; temperature changes—measure with a thermometer to watch for temperature changes; light intensity—ensure same light source is used

[1 mark for each source of error and 1 mark for the associated fix, 6 marks cannot be gained just by listing six problems]

l. i. 15 units

   ii. The line is becoming flat; beyond light intensity of 20 units; another factor is limiting the rate

8 Transpiration

1. a. mm or cm
   b. Furthest end of bubble; reduce error or increase accuracy; bubble has a width
   c. Changing distance; wide range of distances can be used; more data points OR changing speed settings; limited to the number of speed settings on a hair dryer
   d. Experiment undertaken inside; windows shut; door kept shut (not opening and closing); air conditioning off
   e. Continuous data
2. a. Apparatus [at least 1 mark must come from this section]: three identical plants; thermometer; scales
   Method [a maximum of 3 marks can be gained from this section]: record the starting mass of plants; incubate plants for (at least) 6 hours at (at least) three different temperatures; record end mass
   Measurements [at least 1 mark must come from this section]: record start and end mass
   Results [at least 1 mark must come from this section]: calculate percentage change in mass; draw line graph
   b. i.

	Plant 1	Plant 2	Plant 3	Plant 4
Starting mass	22.35	21.40	35.68	19.2
Final mass	21.90	17.12	**32.11**	17.088
% change	−2%	−20%	−10%	−11%

      ii. No units for mass; values given to different resolutions (different number of decimal places)
      iii. Plant 2; lost the largest mass
   c. Gradient of line represents rate of change;
   $$gradient = \frac{change\ in\ y}{change\ in\ x}$$

9 Heart rate

1. a. To get resting heart rate; to compare against
   b. Change the length of time exercised; range of values, for example 1 minute, 2 minutes
   c. i. Exercise stops
      ii. 105 bmp
      iii. 3 minutes
      iv. $\frac{(80 - 60)}{(4 - 2)}; = 10$; bpm^2
      v. Between 3 and 4 minutes; steepest gradient
   d. Any six from: both start increasing when exercise starts (time 0); heart rate reaches a maximum of 145 beats per minute; breathing rate reaches a maximum of 60 breaths per minute; heart rate increases rapidly; heart rate decreases rapidly; heart rate gets back to normal levels quickly; breathing rate increases slowly; breathing rate decreases slowly; breathing rate takes a long time to get back to normal
2. a. Limewater test; for carbon dioxide; goes cloudy if positive
   b. Wear googles; to prevent splash back of limewater; wash hands; if limewater gets on skin; don't blow too vigorously; don't cause limewater to bubble; ensure clips are open/closed at the correct time; so you don't breathe in limewater
   c. Tube A no change; little carbon dioxide in the air; tube B goes cloudy; increased percentage of carbon dioxide in exhaled air
   d. Use a data logger; linked to a computer; record values over time; percentage transmission of light
   e. More carbon dioxide released/more positive result; heavier breathing

10 Respiration

1. a. To increase contrast; to make it easier to see
   b. Method 1; method 1 mixes solutions and then starts the experiments; method 2 misses a large part of the gas released
   c. Keep solutions in water bath while the experiment is carried out; no change in temperature over time; temperature affects rate
   d. At least one temperature between 0 °C and 25 °C; one at room temperature; at least two above room temperature; at least five different temperatures given; range over 40 °C; minimum interval of 10 °C

e.

Time / s	Distance moved by bubble / mm				
	Temperature / °C				
	10	20	30	40	50
30					
60					
90					
120					
150					

f. **i.** Production of carbon dioxide; turning limewater cloudy

    ii. Stop timing when you can no longer see the cross; more accurate

g. **i.** Yeast is living; boiling water would kill it; warm water means it is active

    ii. To ensure it is still alive

h. x-axis is labelled time with units; y-axis is labelled carbon dioxide with units; smooth line; line starts by going up but eventually levels off

11 Tropic responses

1. **a.** $\frac{1}{2}$ mark each from: newly germinated seedlings (for example, mustard seeds); three Petri dishes; cotton wool or compost; water and pipette; small cardboard box (for example, a shoebox); scissors; lamp or light bank; ruler

    b. Temperature; volumes of water given; type of seed

    c. Large seeds so they are easy to handle; quick germination time

    d. Doesn't fit in with lesson time OR weekends/holidays

    e. **i.** 4 marks for getting all answers correct; 3 marks for getting six out of eight correct; deduct 1 mark if anomalous result of seedling 5 has been included in the mean; deduct 1 mark if means are given to more than one decimal place

Day	Height of seedling / cm								
	Seedling number								Mean
	1	2	3	4	5	6	7	8	
1	2	3	4	3	2	1	3	4	2.8
2	3	5	5	4	2	3	4	5	4.1
3	4	6	7	6	3	5	5	5	5.4
4	5	7	9	8	3	7	6	6	6.9
5	7	8	10	9	3	9	7	7	8.1
6	8	10	11	10	3	10	8	8	9.3
7	10	11	12	11	3	11	10	9	10.6

    ii. 100 / 168 = 0.6 mm/hr

    f. 11.2 / 6 = 1.9 cm / day
[1 mark for correct number to one decimal place; 1 mark for units]

    g. For each line: appropriate units and scale on x-axis and y-axis; all points plotted correctly (for both conditions); correct line of best fit

    h. 10.6 cm

    i. Colour of light; direction of light

2. **a.** Qualitative

    b. To make it easier to see the result

    c. As a control; to compare it to

12 Observation and dissection of flowers and seeds

1. **a.** $\frac{1}{2}$ mark for each label; clean lines; continuous lines; no shading

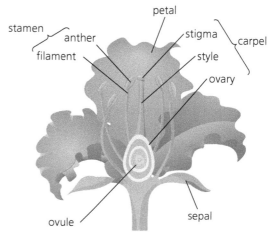

    b. Cork board; sharp blade; keep blade pointing downwards; wear goggles

    c. 14 nm

2. 1 mark each for clean lines; continuous lines; no shading

13 Germination

1. **a.** Stated known volume under 5 cm³; method of measuring stated volume (for example measuring cylinder or pipette)

    b. To prevent the water evaporating; to stop the paper drying out

    c. **i.** 16 / 100 = 0.16; 25 × 0.16 = 4; 25 − 4 = 21 seeds germinated

      ii. 96 / 100 = 0.96; 25 × 0.96 = 24 seeds expected to germinate

    d. Base of dish; lid can be taken off and moved around but base won't

2. **a.** **i.** Water

      ii. Nothing

      iii. Oxygen (gases)

      iv. Light

b. One of the following: count number of seeds germinated; OR height of seeds germinated; measured by ruler

c. Control; check for anomalous result; anomalous results can be excluded; determine average (height not number germinated)

d. Controls volume of water; controls oxygen; states a range of five temperatures; gives a way of controlling temperatures (e.g. location: fridge); gives a way of measuring results (number of seeds germinated or height of seedlings); gives a time period for experiment; gives safety precautions

3. No seeds germinated with abscisic acid; water is needed for germination; after four days approximately 90% of the seeds had germinated (or other data point)

14 Continuous and discontinuous variation

1. a. Discontinuous

b. 10%

2. a. Continuous

b. 15%

c. Histogram

3. Phenotype is a combination of genes and environment; affected by water; affected by soil nutrients; affected by light intensity

4. a. Discontinuous

b. Bar chart

15 Methods of sampling

1. a. A avoids unconscious bias

b. Obtaining an accurate number would take too long

c. 10,000 cm^2

d. 0.25 × 0.25; = 0.0625 m^2

e. i. 30 m × 75 m = 2,250 m^2
0.75 cm × 0.75 cm = 0.5625 m^2
Ignore quadrat 4 result as anomalous
0.5625 m^2 × 9 = 5.0625 m^2
(2,250 / 5.0625) × 165 = 73,333

ii. Mean = 25.4; median = 20

2. a. Predict what effect it would have on habitat; look for rare species that need to be protected

b. Obtaining an accurate number would take too long

c. Sample a greater number of 1 m^2 areas

17 Magnification

1. a. So it doesn't slip as the stage is moved; to ensure the image stays within the viewfinder as observations are taking place

b. If it was moved from lowest to highest, the slide might collide with the lens, breaking the slide (the person viewing is looking down the objective lens and not at the position of the slide); safer; less chance of dangerous material being spilt

c. Wide view; easier to find section to focus on

d.

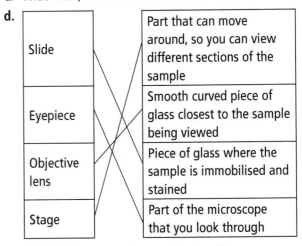

2. a. Onion cells grow underground, where there is no sunlight so no photosynthesis can take place

b. A ×4

c. So accurate measurements can be made

d. Image A: ×400; Image B: ×40; Image C: ×100

e. Start with the lowest (least powerful) objective lens; find sample; adjust focus wheel until it becomes clear and in focus; repeat with higher objective lenses until it is clear

f. C, E, D, A, B

3. a. 12.5 cm

b. Size of real object = $\dfrac{\text{image size}}{\text{magnification}}$

c. 20,000 µm / 400 = 50 µm
[1 mark for correct conversion of cm to µm; 1 mark for correct magnification; 1 mark for answer; answer mark can only be given if units are used]

d. Volume of nucleus = 288 µm^3; volume of whole cell = 1,333,333 µm^3; volume of cell is 4,630 times larger than volume of nucleus; use of µm^3; rounding to whole number correctly [1 mark for each]

e. 13 µm

Title:

Step 1: Make observations

Step 2: Formulate a question

Step 3: Make a hypothesis

Step 4: Conduct experiments

Step 5: Record Results

Step 6: Report Results

Name:	Date:

Title:

Step 1: Make observations	**Step 2: Formulate a question**
Step 3: Make a hypothesis	**Step 4: Conduct experiments**
Step 5: Record Results	**Step 6: Report Results**

Name:	Date:

Title:

Step 1: Make observations

Step 2: Formulate a question

Step 3: Make a hypothesis

Step 4: Conduct experiments

Step 5: Record Results

Step 6: Report Results

Name:

Date:

Title:

Step 1: Make observations

Step 2: Formulate a question

Step 3: Make a hypothesis

Step 4: Conduct experiments

Step 5: Record Results

Step 6: Report Results